Let's Learn About…
Birds!

Curious Toddler Series

Volume 5

Cheryl Shireman

DEDICATION

This book is dedicated to Anna Lee - my favorite toddler.

With much love, Bomb Bomb

Ostrich

Some birds are big.

Hummingbird

Some birds are small.

Owl

An owl sings a song that sounds like "Whoo Whoo."

Morning dove

A morning dove sings a song
that sounds like "Oo-wah-hooo,
hoo hoo."

Parrot

Some birds are many colors.

Flamingo

Some birds are one color.

Robin

A robin has an orange belly.

Bluebird

A bluebird has an orange belly too.

Robin

Some birds live in nests they build in trees.

Bluebird

Some birds live in birdhouses
built by people.

Nest

A nest is made of grass and twigs and holds eggs.

Robin eggs

Baby birds are hatched from the eggs.

Mallard duck

Some birds like to float in the water.

Swan

Some birds stick their heads into the water!

Baby robins

Baby birds say, "Peep peep peep!" when they are hungry.

Robins

Baby birds are fed by their mommy or daddy.

Canada Geese

Some birds don't like the cold winter weather so they fly to warmer places.

Cardinal

Some birds like the cold
weather of winter.

Bluebird splashing

A birdbath gives birds a place
to take a bath.

Goldfinch

A birdfeeder gives birds a
place to eat.

Sandhill Crane

Some birds have very long legs.

Toucan

Some birds have very long beaks.

Bald Eagle

A bald eagle is a very powerful bird and has a white head and tail.

Swan

A swan is a very graceful bird
that lives on lakes.

Baby duck

Some birds are very cute!

Peacock

Some birds are beautiful.

Assorted feathers

A bird's wing is made of many feathers.

Falcon

A bird flies by flapping its wings.

Some birds,

are made just for you!

 The end.

We hope you enjoyed this
Curious Toddler book.

Also in the Curious Toddler series...

Let's Learn About...Dogs!
Let's Learn About...Cats!
Let's Learn About...Things to Drive!
Let's Learn About...Jungle Animals!
Let's Learn About...Birds!
Let's Learn About...Wild Animals!
Let's Learn About...Horses!
Let's Learn About...Farm Animals!

Let's Learn About ...

DOGS !

A CURIOUS TODDLER BOOK

Ages 2-5
Volume 1

Cheryl Shireman

Let's Learn About ...

CATS !

A CURIOUS TODDLER BOOK

Ages 2-5
Volume 2

Cheryl Shireman

Let's Learn About ...

Things to DRIVE !

A CURIOUS TODDLER BOOK

Ages 2-5
Volume 3

Cheryl Shireman

Let's Learn About ...

JUNGLE ANIMALS!

A CURIOUS TODDLER BOOK

Ages 2-5
Volume 4

Cheryl Shireman

Let's Learn About ...

BIRDS!

A CURIOUS TODDLER BOOK

Ages 2-5
Volume 5

Cheryl Shireman

Let's Learn About ...

WILD ANIMALS!

A CURIOUS TODDLER BOOK

Ages 2-5
Volume 6

Cheryl Shireman

Let's Learn About ...

HORSES!

A CURIOUS TODDLER BOOK

Ages 2-5
Volume 7

Cheryl Shireman

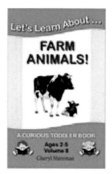

Let's Learn About ...

FARM ANIMALS!

A CURIOUS TODDLER BOOK

Ages 2-5
Volume 8

Cheryl Shireman

ABOUT THE AUTHOR

Cheryl Shireman created the Curious Toddler Series. Cheryl is married and lives in Indiana on a beautiful lake with her husband. She has three grown children and one adorable granddaughter.

Cheryl also writes novels for big people:
Life is But a Dream: On The Lake
Life is But a Dream: In The Mountains
Broken Resolutions
Cooper Moon: The Calling

She is also the author of the beloved non-fiction book, You Don't Need a Prince: A Letter to My Daughter

All of her books can be found online on Amazon.
amazon.com/author/cherylshireman
Her website is www.cherylshireman.com
She can also be found on Twitter and Facebook.

Made in the USA
San Bernardino, CA
16 October 2016